Flowchart Smart

THE SCIENCE OF RAIN FORESTS

Richard and Louise Spilsbury

Gareth Stevens PUBLISHING

Please visit our website, **www.garethstevens.com**.
For a free color catalog of all our high-quality books,
call toll free 1-800-542-2595 or fax 1-877-542-2596.

Cataloging-in-Publication Data

Names: Spilsbury, Richard. | Spilsbury, Louise.
Title: Rain forests / Richard and Louise Spilsbury.
Description: New York : Gareth Stevens Publishing, 2020. | Series: Flowchart smart | Includes glossary and index.
Identifiers: ISBN 9781538252314 (pbk.) | ISBN 9781538252321 (library bound)
Subjects: LCSH: Rain forests--Juvenile literature. | Rain forest ecology--Juvenile literature.
Classification: LCC QH86.S65 2020 | DDC 577.34--dc23

First Edition

Published in 2020 by
Gareth Stevens Publishing
111 East 14th Street, Suite 349
New York, NY 10003

Produced for Gareth Stevens by Calcium
Editors: Sarah Eason and Harriet McGregor
Designer: Emma DeBanks
Picture researcher: Rachel Blount

Picture credits: Cover: Shutterstock: Maquiladora (br), Tayka Ya (c); Inside: Shutterstock: A-t-i: p. 12b; Gudkov Andrey: pp. 34-35, 45r; Galyna Andrushko: pp. 10-11; Jomar Aplaon: pp. 16-17; Agnieszka Bacal: p. 23t; Rich Carey: pp. 40-41; Nuttavut Chakthranont: p. 15r; Norma Cornes: pp. 18-19; Danita Delmont: pp. 7t, 36b; Dirk Ercken: p. 21r; Steffen Foerster: p. 34b; GraphicsRF: pp. 42-43; Anastasiia Lieonova: pp. 20-21; Maquiladora: p. 39; Mazur Travel: pp. 12-13; Parkol: p. 29; Jamey Penney-Ritter: p. 25; Phungatanee: p. 26b; Dr Morley Read: p. 11t; Matyas Rehak: pp. 26-27; Rhoeo: pp. 32-33; Luiz C. Ribeiro: pp. 30-31; SaveJungle: p. 9; Vaclav Sebek: pp. 22-23; Fedor Selivanov: pp. 1, 19r; Sharp: pp. 36-37; Szefei: p. 5b; Markus Thomanek: p. 41t; Lillian Tveit: p. 28b; Unique Vision: pp. 6-7; Richard Whitcombe: pp. 4-5; Somrerk Witthayanant: pp. 44-45; Worldclassphoto: p. 31t; Zulashai: p. 15r.

Printed in the United States of America

CPSIA compliance information: Batch #CW20GS: For further information contact Gareth Stevens, New York, New York at 1-800-542-2595.

Contents

Chapter 1

What Are Rain Forests?

Rain forests are lush, healthy forests. These amazing **ecosystems** are home to around half of all Earth's plants and animals.

An ecosystem is made up of all of the living and nonliving things that **interact** with each other in an area. It includes living things such as plants and animals and nonliving things, such as the weather, sunlight, water, and soil. All ecosystems have their own unique features. The rain forest ecosystem includes everything in the rain forest, from the tiniest drops of water to large rain forest animals such as jaguars.

A covering of clouds hangs over this rain forest, ready to drop rain on the huge, damp ecosystem.

As their name suggests, the most significant nonliving feature of these rain forest ecosystems is the amount of water they receive. Rain forests are usually found in regions where there is a high annual rainfall of generally more than 70 inches (178 cm) per year. The climate in these ecosystems is warm and steamy, and most rain forest soils are moist. The warmth, sunlight, water, and air in a rain forest allow plants to grow easily. The main plants in rain forests are tall, broad-leaved trees that tower above the land.

Get Smart!

The largest rain forests on Earth are found around the Amazon River in South America and the Congo River in Africa. There are also rain forests in West and Central Africa, on islands in Southeast Asia, and in parts of Australia. The **evergreen** forests of North America's Pacific Northwest and Northern Europe are a type of rain forest. There are also rain forests in parts of Japan, New Zealand, and other parts of South America.

The ground of this tropical rain forest in Southeast Asia is thickly covered by plants of all sizes.

Temperate and Tropical

There are two types of rain forest in the world: **temperate rain forests** and **tropical rain forests**. Although they are found in different places, they share certain characteristics.

Most rain forests grow in the tropics. The tropics are found to the north and south of the equator, an imaginary line around the center of Earth. In this region, it is hot and sunny and rains almost every day. The air is usually humid, or damp, because the sun's heat **evaporates** water, turning it rapidly from a liquid into a gas called **water vapor**. Tropical rain forests can have 100 different types of trees per square mile, including fig, mahogany, and eucalyptus trees.

Get Smart!

Tropical rain forests are so warm and moist that they produce as much as 75 percent of their own rain. The heat evaporates water from the surface of the trees' leaves. More water then moves from the stems into the leaves through narrow tubes. This movement pulls water from the roots into the tubes. This allows the tree roots to move water from the damp soil into their roots. As the water vapor in the air rises, it cools and **condenses** into clouds. It falls back to the ground as rain.

This tropical rain forest is in Thailand, in Southeast Asia.

Coastal temperate rain forests, such as the Great Bear Rainforest in British Columbia, comprise only 2–3 percent of the world's rain forests.

Temperate rain forests are found in cooler parts of Earth. These ecosystems often have dry summers and cold, wet winters. These weather conditions are created by high coastal mountains that trap moisture-laden clouds moving inland from the ocean. The clouds bring heavy rains. Alongside the mild temperatures, this rainfall encourages the rapid growth of trees. Trees typically seen in temperate rain forests include cedars, redwoods, laurel, and cypresses, which are usually less dense and not as tall as those found in a tropical rain forest.

Get flowchart smart!

How Rain Forests Make Rain

Let's discover how tropical rain forests make their own rain.

The heat in a tropical rain forest causes water on the surface of leaves to evaporate.

Water vapor in the air rises, cools, and condenses into clouds.

It falls back to the ground as rain.

More water moves into the leaves from the stems, through narrow tubes.

This movement pulls water from the roots into the tubes.

This helps the tree roots move water into their roots from the damp soil.

Flowchart Smart

Chapter 2

Rain Forest Plants

Plants in the rain forest can grow bigger and faster than anywhere else in the world. Some tropical rain forest trees—such as teak, mahogany, and rosewood—can grow incredibly tall.

The top layer of the rain forest is called the emergent layer. This is where the tallest trees emerge above the main forest. Trees here can grow to more than 200 feet (60 m) high. Rain forest soils are very thin and trees here must have shallow roots in order to absorb, or soak up, **nutrients** from them. These roots are too shallow to keep the trees upright, so they have big, wide buttress roots that grow aboveground. They flare out at the base of the tree and look a little like stilts. They help prop up the tree.

Temperate rain forests in the Pacific Northwest are home to giant conifers, some of them more than 300 feet (90 m) tall and 1,000 years old.

Beneath the emergent layer is the canopy. Trees here grow to about 100 feet (30 m) above the ground. Their thick layers of leaves and branches form a canopy, or roof, over the ground, blocking sunlight and making the forest below dark. Most canopy trees have smooth, oval leaves that come to a point called a drip tip. This shape allows water to run off the leaves quickly without damaging or breaking them.

The buttress roots on some tropical rain forest trees can extend 30 feet (9 m) around the trunk.

Get Smart!

In temperate rain forests, large cone-bearing conifer trees form a canopy over the forest. Some temperate rain forest conifers, such as redwoods and giant sequoias in California, can live for thousands of years. They are some of the biggest living things on the planet. Other trees, such as hornbeam or dogwood, live for far less time and are much shorter, barely reaching the canopy.

Among the Trees

Plants need access to water, nutrients, and sunlight to be able to grow and survive. Beneath the canopy, smaller trees and other plants have some smart ways of ensuring they receive a share of these **resources**.

In a dense forest, the canopy trees can block out more than 95 percent of the sunlight, so shrubs and smaller trees below the canopy, such as palms, have giant leaves. This helps them make sure they catch as much light that filters through from above as possible. The leaves on these trees are also often arranged at certain angles so that they avoid shading their own leaves, which would reduce the amount of light they receive.

These rain forest leaves have a large surface area across which they absorb sunlight.

Some plants take a shortcut to the top of tall rain forest trees and branches to get the light they need. Epiphytes such as some ferns and orchids can grow on other plants. Some have feathery or dustlike seeds that get carried easily on the wind and blow onto high branches, where they begin to grow. Some produce fruits that animals pick and climb into trees to eat, leaving seeds behind, high in the tree. The seeds often germinate in pockets of rotting plant waste. They get some of the nutrients they need to grow from this plant matter. They dangle their roots in the air to get the water they need, which is why epiphytes are often called air plants.

The giant tropical rain forest plant rafflesia has no leaves and no stem, but it does have one of the biggest flowers in the world.

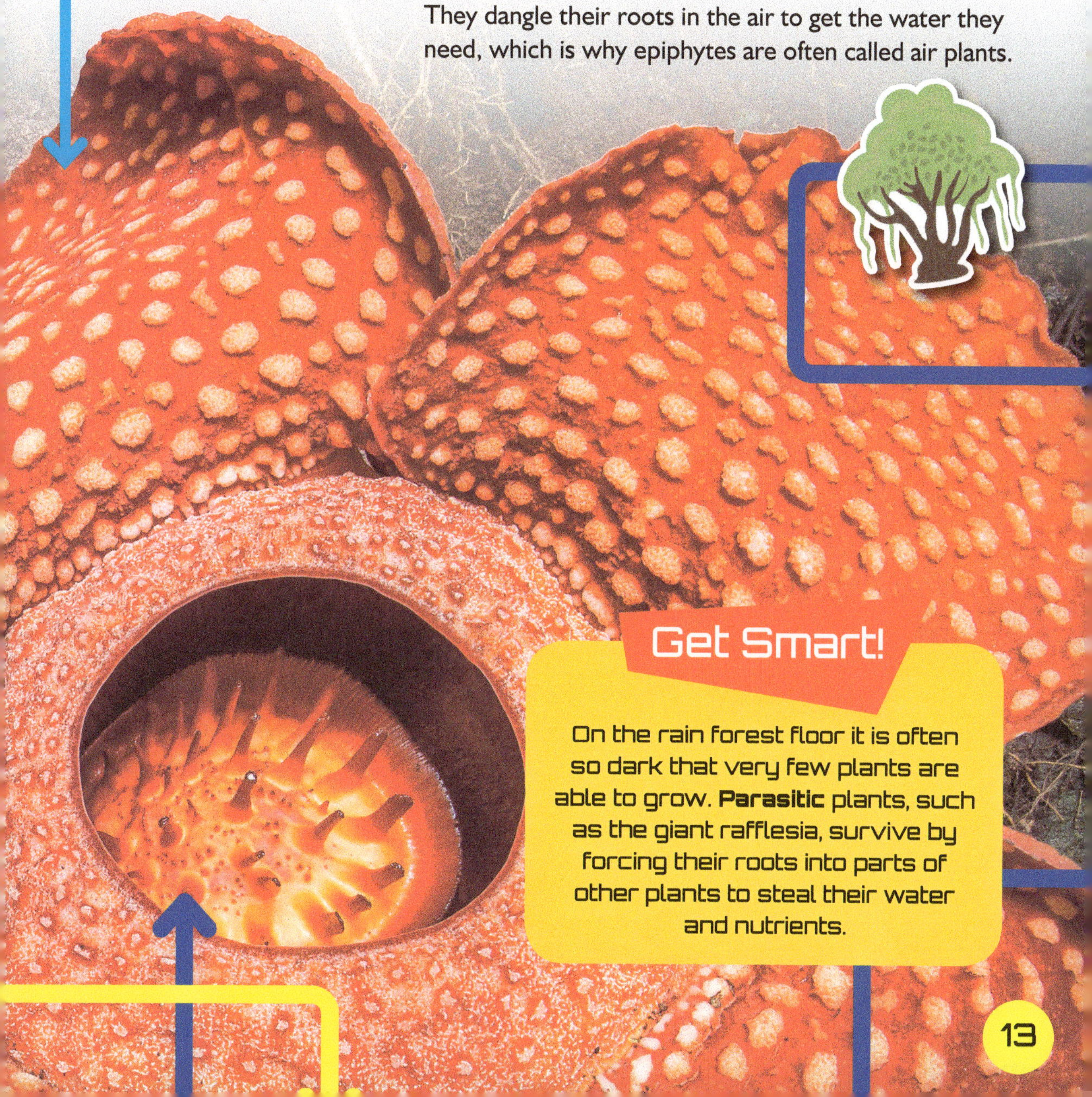

Get Smart!

On the rain forest floor it is often so dark that very few plants are able to grow. **Parasitic** plants, such as the giant rafflesia, survive by forcing their roots into parts of other plants to steal their water and nutrients.

Cunning Climbers

Some plants compete for precious resources in the rain forest by wrapping themselves around trees and using the tree trunks for support. Some even destroy the **host** tree in the process.

Around 90 percent of the world's vine species grow in tropical rain forests. Vines have roots in the ground, and slender stems that twist around tree trunks to climb upward. Liana vines are thick, woody vines that can grow as long as 3,000 feet (914 m). When lianas reach the light at the top, they grow colorful flowers.

Get Smart!

Vine stems have different methods of gripping the rain forest tree trunks. Some wind themselves around very tightly. Others have threadlike parts growing from their stems called tendrils, which can clasp surfaces. Others have thorns or spikes that attach the vine to its host, or even sticky hairs that point downward, keeping the vine stuck to its host.

These big jungle lianas have twisted their way up the high rain forest trees.

The strangler fig begins life as a seed in the top of a tree. As it grows, it sends roots down to the forest floor by wrapping them around the host tree. The roots grow into and take nutrients and water from the soil. This helps the roots grow thicker and thicker until they merge together, forming a dense network around the host tree. These roots squeeze the host tree's trunk so tightly that they stop water and nutrients from flowing up inside it. The fig tree's leaves also grow above the host tree and starve it of light. The strangler fig steals all the resources the host tree needs, and it eventually dies.

There are almost 2,500 species of vines. These smaller vines cling closely to the stem of rain forest plants to get closer to the light.

Get flowchart smart!

How a Strangler Fig Kills Trees

Let's find out how and why a strangler fig kills rain forest trees.

The strangler fig begins life as a seed in the top of a tree.

The fig tree's leaves also grow above the host tree, starving it of light.

The strangler fig takes all the resources the host tree needs, so it dies.

When the host tree dies and rots away, the fig tree is left growing in its place.

As it grows, it sends roots down to the forest floor by wrapping them around the host tree.

The roots grow into and take nutrients and water from the soil.

This helps the roots grow thicker and thicker until they merge together, forming a dense network around the host tree.

The roots squeeze the host tree's trunk so tightly that they stop water and nutrients from flowing up inside it.

Flowchart Smart

Chapter 3

Animal Adaptations

Some animals have amazing **adaptations** that help them survive the challenges of living in a rain forest ecosystem.

A behavioral adaptation is a way of acting, or behaving, that helps a living thing survive in its ecosystem. Chimpanzees have learned to use several different tools to get their food and water. They crunch up soft leaves and use them like sponges to soak up water from inside fallen tree trunks to drink. They break, bite, and twist twigs to form particular shapes, lengths, and thicknesses. Then they poke them into holes in tree trunks to scoop out termites and ants, which they quickly wipe into their mouths before the bugs can bite. Chimps also use stick tools to scoop honey from bees' nests to avoid getting stung.

Get Smart!

Some birds travel very long distances to find food. They usually have long, pointed wings. However, in the rain forest, there is plenty of food, so birds do not have to travel far. Their wings are shorter and rounder, which helps them maneuver quickly between trees and shrubs in the rain forest.

Chimps are so good at using and making tools that they have even been seen joining two sticks together to make a longer tool for reaching up high or into places.

A physical adaptation is a body feature that helps an animal survive. Some of the fruits and nuts in a rain forest have very hard coverings and shells. Parrots, macaws, and toucans are birds that have adapted to eat this food by developing a long, large, and very strong beak that serves as a nutcracker. The toucan's beak is so long that it also helps it reach and cut fruit and nuts from branches that are too weak to support its weight. The other advantage of a large beak is that it can make a very loud noise. This is an advantage in the rain forest, where birds have to communicate over long distances through a large area of dense trees.

A toucan's beak can be four times the size of its head and almost as long as its body.

Masters of Disguise

Some rain forest animals use disguises to blend in with rain forest trees and other plants. Some use this ability to keep safe, and others use it to help them find and attack prey, or animals that they eat.

This giant leaf-tailed gecko is very hard to spot on a rain forest tree.

Stick insects hide from predators, or animals that hunt and eat them, by blending into the plants they live on. They look just like sticks, and some even sway to and fro so that they look like a twig moving gently in the wind. Walking stick insects blend in so well with the palm trees they live on that it is almost impossible to see them until they move. Some butterflies have patterns on their wings that make them look exactly like bark or leaves when they close their wings to rest on a twig or branch.

Camouflage can also be used to help predators catch their prey. A jaguar's yellowish-brown fur has patches and spots on it that help it blend in with the leaves on the rain forest floor. Giant leaf-tailed geckos use their camouflage to lie in wait and ambush unsuspecting insects and other prey as they crawl up trees. The mottled brownish color of their body blends in with the branch, and fringed flaps on their lower jaws and the sides of their body can flatten against the bark, making its outline disappear.

The red strawberry poison dart frog's colors warn predators that it is poisonous.

Get Smart!

Poison dart frogs have poison on their skin. They are brightly colored to warn potential predators not to eat them because they are dangerous. Some frogs that are not poisonous have adapted to their ecosystem by having bright colors, too. Their colors help them pretend to be poisonous to keep them from being eaten by predators.

On the Move

Rain forest trees are very tall, so animals must move between them carefully. Dropping from high branches could be fatal.

Gibbons swing along from branch to branch using their incredibly powerful arms and shoulders. Some monkeys have tails that can curl around branches, allowing the monkey to hold on to the tree with its tail. Sloths slowly move through the branches hanging upside-down from long, curved claws. Many tree frogs have cup-shaped toes that help them suction themselves to the underside of leaves, where they rest during the day. The toes also help them cling to tree bark.

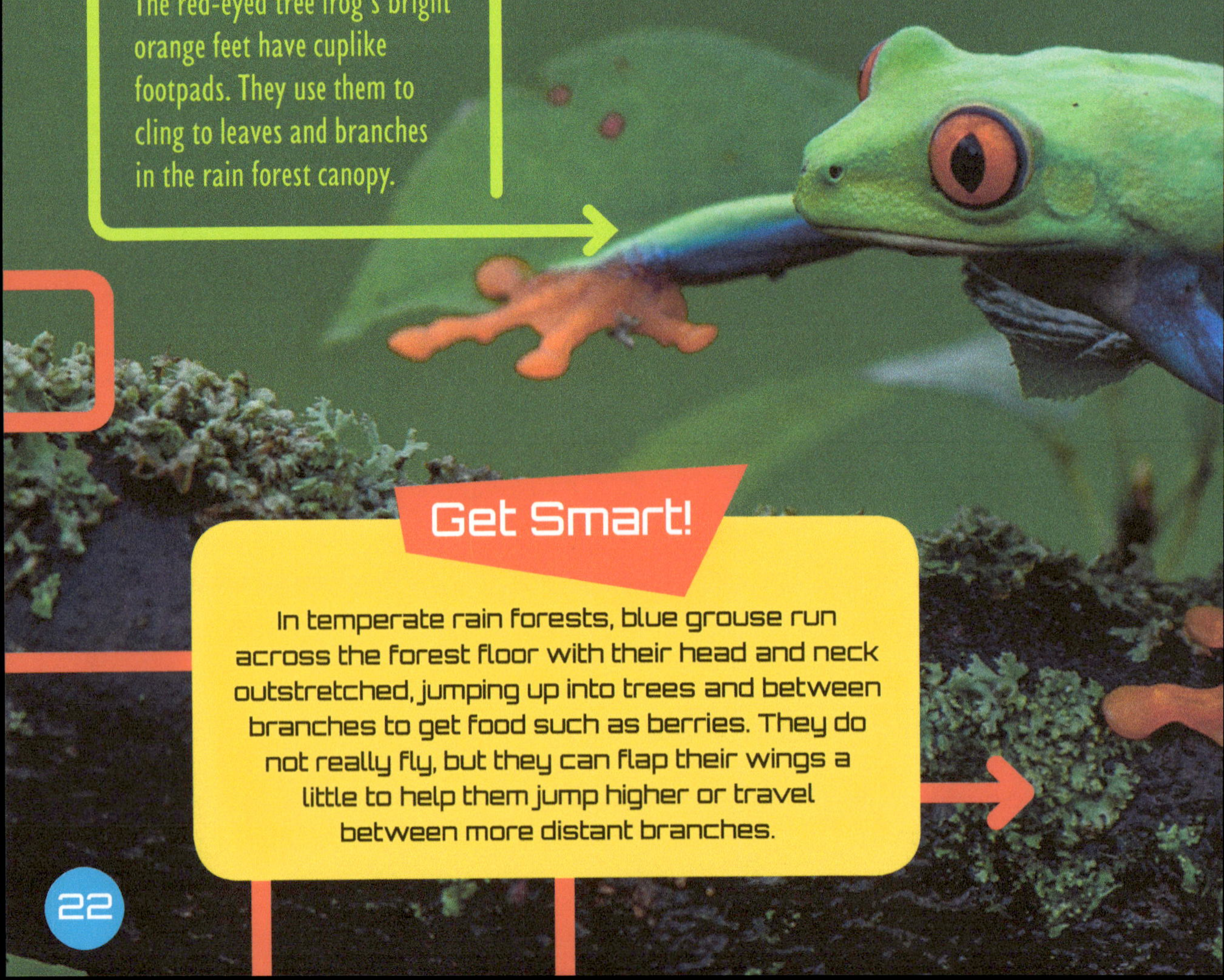

The red-eyed tree frog's bright orange feet have cuplike footpads. They use them to cling to leaves and branches in the rain forest canopy.

Get Smart!

In temperate rain forests, blue grouse run across the forest floor with their head and neck outstretched, jumping up into trees and between branches to get food such as berries. They do not really fly, but they can flap their wings a little to help them jump higher or travel between more distant branches.

Flying squirrels that live high in rain forest treetops do not actually fly; they glide. As the squirrel launches itself from one tree, it spreads out its arms and legs to stretch the loose extra skin between its wrists and ankles into a square shape. The extra skin acts as a parachute so the animal can be carried gently by the wind. Flying squirrels usually glide down from one branch to a lower branch on another tree. They scurry to the top of that tree, and then jump from there onto another.

A flying squirrel can glide up to 300 feet (91 m) from tree to tree.

Get flowchart smart!

How Flying Squirrels "Fly"

Discover how a flying squirrel "flies" between trees in a rain forest.

When a flying squirrel launches itself from a tree, it spreads out its arms and legs.

The flying squirrel usually glides down from one branch to a lower branch on another tree. It scurries to the top of that tree, and then jumps from there onto another.

This stretches out the loose extra skin between its wrists and ankles into a square shape.

The extra skin acts as a parachute so the animal can be carried gently by the wind.

Chapter 4

Food Chains

The lives of all the living things in a rain forest are linked together in many different food chains, which all begin with plants and trees.

Trees get their energy from the sun. Like other green plants, they are adapted for making their own food by **photosynthesis**. Leaves trap the energy from sunlight. This energy is used to turn **carbon dioxide** and water into sugars. The tree uses the sugars to grow. In rain forest food chains, plants are the **producers**. They are first in the food chain because they produce their own food.

Many animals feed on the leaves, fruit, seeds, and other parts of rain forest plants. These animals are known as **consumers** because they have to consume food from outside their bodies to survive. Leafcutter ants use leaves to grow fungi to eat. First, they cut off pieces of leaf with their powerful jaws. They carry them back to their nest. Here, ants chew the leaves and release substances that encourage fungi to grow on the leafy mush. Other ants in the **colony** keep the fungi farm growing well. Finally, the ants eat the fungi and also feed it to the young larvae in the nest.

Get Smart!

When plants use photosynthesis to make their own food, they release **oxygen** as a waste product. Oxygen is a gas in the air that almost all living things need to survive. Rain forests are vital oxygen factories. They produce about 40 percent of the planet's oxygen.

A leafcutter ant can carry a piece of leaf up to 50 times its own body weight. That is like a man carrying a van!

The giant taro leaf can reach over 6 feet (2 m) long. Thick stems 4 inches (10 cm) wide hold the leaves up toward the sunlight.

Finding Food

Rain forest animals find food both in the trees and on the forest floor. Some eat a wide variety of plant foods. Others have very smart ways of ensuring they get enough to eat.

Orangutans eat more than 400 different types of food. They mainly feed on ripe fruit, but also eat young leaves, bark, flowers, honey, insects, vines, and the inner shoots of plants. Green iguanas climb on branches, eating leaves and fruit from the trees using their strong jaws and razor-sharp teeth. They can grow to 3 feet (1 m) long. Green iguanas can snap their tails like a whip if an animal tries to catch and eat them. The tail can also break off if caught by a predator, without harming the iguana.

Some animals that live on the forest floor, such as agoutis, a type of rodent, follow monkeys and parrots to find food. They eat the fruits and nuts dropped by these animals from high in the treetops. Armadillos shuffle along the rain forest floor on their short legs using their long, pointed noses and long, sticky tongues to catch insects. They can consume up to 40,000 ants in one meal. Armadillos also feed on small animals, bird eggs, roots, and fruits.

One of the orangutan's favorite fruits is the durian. The fruit has a very strong smell and tastes a little like a cheesy custard.

Get Smart!

In temperate rain forests, most animals find their food on the forest floor, where there are small plants, grass, and plenty of insects. Lichens that grow high in the canopy fall to the ground where they are eaten by animals, including elk. Black bears have long claws that help them dig into rotten trunks to unearth beetle larvae to eat.

Armadillos have a leathery, armor-like covering and long, sharp claws for digging up insects to eat.

Predators

Predators are at the top of the rain forest food chains. Large predators track, chase, and catch animals that eat plants and they eat smaller predators too.

Harpy eagles are apex, or top, predators of the tropical rain forest. These powerful birds rest on high perches on the lookout for a meal. They swoop down at high speed, snatching prey up with their large feet. After carrying the prey to a high branch, they use their sharp, hooked beak to tear off pieces of meat to swallow. Harpy eagles mainly feed on plant-eating animals such as sloths, monkeys, macaws, and reptiles such as iguanas.

Jaguars are rain forest hunters. They can climb trees and catch prey, and can even swim in rain forest rivers. They leap onto their prey and have teeth sharp enough to pierce an animal's skull and kill it with a single bite. They can even stalk and kill anacondas, one of the biggest and deadliest snakes in the ecosystem. One of the animals anacondas eat are peccaries. An anaconda kills its prey by coiling its body around the creature and squeezing until the animal can no longer breathe. Peccaries are a type of wild pig that likes to gobble up plant-eating insects and lizards for dinner.

The harpy eagle has large, forward-facing eyes to spot prey. The feathers around its face help funnel sounds to its ears and help it hear better.

This anaconda has seized a fish in its giant jaws and is about to eat it.

Get Smart!

Sometimes, several different animals eat the same foods. Iguanas are eaten by a variety of natural predators including hawks, owls, and snakes. Many food chains linked together are called a **food web**.

Get flowchart smart!

A Jaguar Rain Forest Food Chain

Let's take a look at a jaguar's food chain.

Rain forest plants trap the sun's energy in their leaves and make their own food inside their bodies.

Jaguars eat anacondas. A jaguar's sharp teeth can pierce the skull of an anaconda and kill it with a single bite.

Ants and other insects eat leaves that fall from the plants to get energy.

Peccaries, a type of wild rain forest pig, eat plant-eating insects.

Anacondas, a type of snake, eat peccaries. An anaconda kills its prey by coiling its body around the creature and squeezing until the animal can no longer breathe.

Flowchart Smart

Chapter 5

Rain Forest Interactions

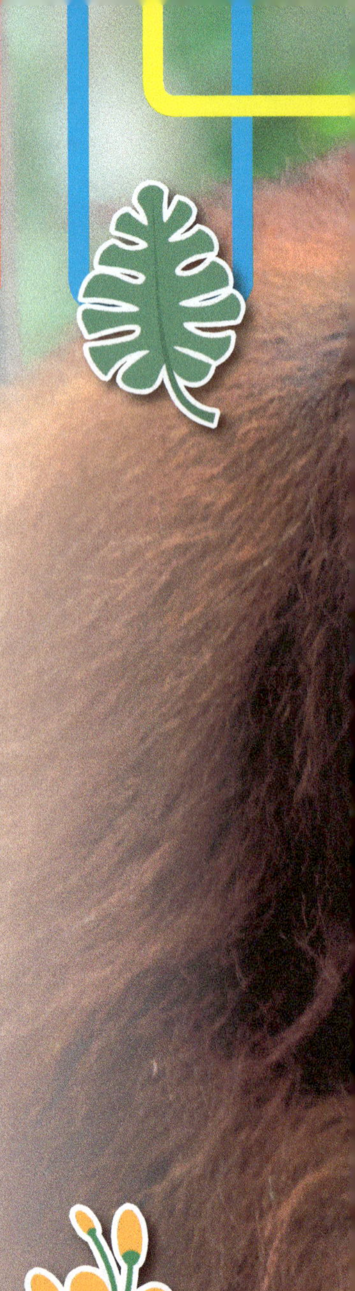

The different living and nonliving parts of a rain forest ecosystem are interconnected. They rely on one another to keep healthy.

Birds and animals eat fruit from trees. In turn, the fruit trees depend upon these animals to help them disperse, or spread, their seeds to distant parts of the forest. Orangutans have a special role in seed dispersal. The seeds from the ripe fruit they eat are excreted in the orangutan feces. The feces also contain nutrients and act as a fertilizer to help the seeds germinate, or start to grow. Orangutans also affect the ecosystem because they grasp and sometimes snap off branches as they travel through the forest canopy. This creates gaps in the plant cover that let light through to the forest floor, allowing other plants to grow.

Rain forest ecosystems also have their own waste disposal system to help them keep healthy. Rain forests are packed with **decomposers**. These are living things that break down large quantities of dead leaves and animal waste. Scavengers, such as millipedes, eat this waste, and fungi decompose what is left. In temperate rain forests, banana slugs are essential **recyclers**. They feed on leaves, mushrooms, and dead animals. This releases nutrients from them, which helps trees grow.

Banana slugs live on the forest floors of the Pacific Northwest. They spread seeds while they eat.

Get Smart!

Strangler figs kill some trees, but they help other plants and animals survive. This makes them a keystone species. A keystone species is one that plays an essential part in an ecosystem. The rotting wood of a host tree killed by a strangler fig is a useful source of nutrients for the soil. Strangler figs also produce fruit several times a year that forest animals such as monkeys and parrots eat. In turn, these animals are vital foods for predators including jaguars and harpy eagles.

Orangutans spit out the seeds of many fruits they eat, helping to disperse the seeds to new places.

Helping Out

In the rain forest, some types of plants and animals have developed relationships with one another that benefit everyone.

Cecropia trees and Azteca ants help one another out. The trees have hollow stems in which the Aztecas can nest. The trees' young leaves make tiny white blobs of sugar-rich food, which the ants eat. In return, the ants protect the trees from predators. They patrol the leafy parts of the tree and drive off leaf-eating insects, such as leafcutter ants, to prevent them from damaging the leaves that both the ants and the tree need.

The three-toed sloth has an amazing relationship with both moths and algae. Once a week, a sloth climbs slowly down from the trees to drop its feces on the forest floor. Moths lay eggs in the dung pile. The moth larvae hatch out of the eggs and live in the dung as they grow. As adults, the moths fly up into the trees to live and shelter in the sloth's fur. The moths add nutrients to the fur, which algae can feed on. The green algae provide camouflage for the sloth's fur. Sloths also eat the algae to supplement their diet of leaves.

Elk are often called the "landscape gardeners" of the temperate rain forest because their feeding and trampling habits are so important to the ecosystem.

Sloths live in the rain forest canopy in Central and South America.

Get Smart!

Elk rely on the plants in a temperate rain forest for food. The plants rely on elk to keep them healthy. Herds of elk trample plants with their hooves. They also eat a lot of plant matter. This keeps the forest healthy by keeping it from becoming too overgrown.

Get flowchart smart!

Sloths, Moths, and Algae

Let's learn how sloths, moths, and algae help one another in a rain forest ecosystem.

Once a week, a sloth climbs slowly down from the trees to drop its feces on the forest floor.

The green algae provide camouflage for the sloth. The sloths also eat the algae to supplement their diet of leaves.

Moths lay eggs in the dung pile.

The moth larvae hatch from the eggs and live in the dung pile as they grow.

As adults, the moths fly up into the trees to live and shelter in the sloth's fur.

The moths add nutrients to the fur. Algae feed on the nutrients.

Flowchart Smart

Chapter 6

The Future of Rain Forest Ecosystems

A rain forest ecosystem exists in a delicate balance. Because the nonliving and living parts in an ecosystem are interconnected, changing one part can put the entire ecosystem out of balance and under threat.

Across the world, the equivalent of 27 soccer fields of forests are destroyed every minute.

The main threat to rain forests is **habitat** destruction. People cut down rain forests to clear land and provide more space for planting crops or for grazing farm animals. Some are destroyed to build highways and mines, or to make space for buildings as towns and cities expand. Trees are also cut down to make products such as windows, doors, tables, and paper. The destruction of forests is called **deforestation**.

A big problem with deforestation is that fewer trees mean that less photosynthesis takes place. Less carbon dioxide is removed from the **atmosphere**. Burning or cutting down trees and leaving them to rot on the forest floor causes carbon stored inside the trees (after they use carbon dioxide during photosynthesis) to be released. This carbon goes back into the atmosphere as carbon dioxide. Carbon dioxide is one of the gases responsible for **climate change**. Burning **fossil fuels** also releases carbon dioxide into the atmosphere. Climate change is causing a gradual rise in the average temperatures across the world.

Climate change is likely to affect the rainfall pattern in rain forests. Plants and animals that cannot adapt to these changes will be in danger and may die out.

Get Smart!

Climate change is causing a lot of problems. **Glaciers** and sea ice are melting and sea levels are rising. This will flood islands and coasts. Oceans are getting warmer, **coral reefs** are dying, and food chains are being damaged. Seasons are changing and extreme weather events such as hurricanes are becoming more common.

Get flowchart smart!

Deforestation and Climate change

Discover how damaging rain forest ecosystems is affecting climate change.

Deforestation occurs when large areas of forest are cut down or burned.

Carbon dioxide is one of the gases responsible for climate change. Climate change is causing a gradual rise in average temperatures across the world. Sea levels are rising and natural habitats are suffering.

When there are fewer trees, less photosynthesis takes place. Less carbon dioxide is removed from the atmosphere.

Burning or cutting down trees and leaving them to rot on the forest floor causes carbon stored inside the trees to be released. This carbon goes back into the atmosphere as carbon dioxide.

Protecting Rain Forest Ecosystems

People all around the world are working in different ways to protect the world's rain forest ecosystems.

Governments help protect rain forest ecosystems by creating areas in which people are not allowed to cut down too many trees or take away natural resources. These protected places are often called **national parks** or reserves. Areas of forest are surrounded by fences and people called rangers keep watch for people who might try to cut down trees illegally. Some countries are working to restore damaged rain forest ecosystems by planting trees on land where forests have been cut down.

These people are planting trees on land where forests have been cut down. This is one way to save the world's precious rain forests.

Get Smart!

Rain forests are destroyed to create land on which cattle and other farm animals can be raised, in order to produce beef for foods such as burgers. You can help the rain forests by eating less meat. Instead, try to choose other protein-rich foods such as beans.

People can make a difference, too, by using fewer natural resources and recycling others. People help the rain forests by buying only recycled paper and secondhand wooden furniture. This reduces the need to cut down new trees. Palm oil is used in many products, and palm oil trees are grown on land cleared by deforestation. You can help by encouraging your family to choose products that do not contain palm oil. You can also help rain forests by asking your family and friends to avoid wood products made from precious rain forest woods, including ebony and rosewood. Rain forests ecosystems are essential to the health of our planet. We should all do all we can to help them have a healthy future.

Animals such as mountain gorillas can live safely in rain forests when they become reserves.

Glossary

adaptations Changes to suit a new situation.

atmosphere The blanket of gases that surrounds Earth.

camouflage The ability to blend in with the surroundings.

carbon dioxide A gas in the air.

climate change A change in the pattern of the world's weather caused by Earth's atmosphere getting warmer.

colony A group of living things such as ants.

condenses Cools and turns from a gas into a liquid.

consumers Animals that eat plants or other animals.

coral reefs Natural structures in warm oceans made from coral animals.

decomposers Living things that break down waste.

deforestation The destruction and removal of forest.

ecosystems The living and nonliving things in a place, interacting with one another.

evaporates Turns from a liquid into a gas.

evergreen A plant that retains its green leaves all year round.

food web The feeding relationships between food chains in an ecosystem.

fossil fuels Coal, oil, or natural gas formed from the remains of living things that died millions of years ago.

glaciers Very slow-moving rivers of ice.

habitat The place where plants and animals live.

host A living thing on which another animal or plant lives.

interact Act in such a way as to have an effect on one another.

national parks Areas in nature where the wildlife is protected by law.

nutrients Substances that living things need to survive and grow.

oxygen A gas found in air and water that animals need to survive.

parasitic Something that lives in or on another and takes nourishment from it.

photosynthesis The process by which green plants make sugary food using the energy in sunlight.

producers Living things that make their own food inside their body.

recyclers Something that turns waste into something new.

resources Things that are useful to people; natural resources include plants and water.

temperate rain forests Rain forests found in places with a moderate range of temperatures.

tropical rain forests Rain forests found in places near the equator that are warm all year round.

water vapor The gas form of water.

For More Information

Books

Dellaccio, Tanya. *Changing Rainforest Environments* (Human Impact on Earth: Cause and Effect). New York, NY: PowerKids Press, 2019.

Gibbs, Maddie. *What Are Tropical Rainforests?* (Let's Find Out! Biomes). New York, NY: Rosen Publishing, 2019.

Hudak, Heather C., *Map and Track Rainforests* (Map and Track Biomes and Animals). New York, NY: Crabtree Publishing Company, 2019.

Watson, Galadriel. *Amazon Rain Forest* (Natural Wonders of the World). New York, NY: Weigl, 2013.

Websites

Visit NASA's Earth Observatory website to find out more about the differences between temperate and tropical rain forests:
earthobservatory.nasa.gov/experiments/biome/biorainforest.php

Discover fun facts about rain forests at this website:
www.natgeokids.com/uk/discover/geography/physical-geography/15-cool-things-about-rainforests

Learn more about the world's biggest rain forest at:
wwf.panda.org/knowledge_hub/where_we_work/amazon/about_the_amazon/ecosystems_amazon/rainforests

Click on the headings to learn all about rain forests at:
www.srl.caltech.edu/personnel/krubal/rainforest/Edit560s6/www/what.html

Index